Awareness Inside Language

Awareness Inside Language

—॥॥—

GEORGE QUASHA

IN CONVERSATION WITH

THOMAS FINK

MATRICES #1

We gratefully acknowledge Jacket2
(Kelly Writers House, 3805 Locust Walk, Philadelphia, PA 19104-6150)
which published "Awareness Inside Language" online in 2016 at
https://jacket2.org/interviews/awareness-inside- language.

MATRICES
is a series of short interim editions of poetics thinking,
published under the auspices of
Station Hill of Barrytown,
a project of the Institute for Publishing Arts, Inc.,
a not-for-profit tax-exempt corporation, 501(c)(3),
120 Station Hill Road
Barrytown, NY 12507

www.stationhill.org

Design and typesetting: Susan Quasha

ISBN: 978-1-58177-171-8

Printed in the United States of America

Awareness Inside Language

Preface

After reading several of George Quasha's collections of "preverb" poems with great interest, I was intrigued by his development of this new poetic mode, the way it shaped the organization of his work over a substantial period of time and the persistent metapoetic (even metalinguistic) thrust of the poetry. George kindly consented to engage in an exchange, and we limited the discussion to four of his preverb books. The interview took place via email from January 8 to February 23, 2016.

— THOMAS FINK

Awareness inside Language

George Quasha and Thomas Fink

The four books under consideration are:

Verbal Paradise (preverbs), Tenerife, Spain: Zasterle Press, 2011

Glossodelia Attract (preverbs), Barrytown, New York: Station Hill of Barrytown, 2015

Things Done for Themselves (preverbs), East Rockaway, New York: Marsh Hawk Press, 2015

The Daimon of the Moment (preverbs), Northfield, Massachusetts: Talisman House Press, 2015

—⁂—

Thomas Fink: In the "pre play" to *Verbal Paradise*, you refer to the preverb as a "kledomantic gathering of stray language according to a singularity-centered principle of organization"[1] and go on to say that these enactments of singularity work "for the public good" by promoting "the destabilization of naming" (ix), which is valuable in a culture that names things and concepts too simply and often coercively. I couldn't find the word "kledomantic" anywhere, but I think that this notion of destabilization is familiar to those who have been involved with the reading and/or writing of innovative poetry; in "pre gnoetic," which is placed after the preverb poems of *The Daimon of the Moment*, you write: "The role of poetry is to do what language can't, or won't, otherwise do" (132). You identify the preverb as a "one-line utterance projecting a particular state of language in the act of finding itself here and now" (134). Like the proverb—we will get to your precursor Blake later—a preverb honors "the impulse to *say* what's true" but also evades "the inevitable limitation of thinking one knows the truth" (134). Let's take five examples of metacognitive utterances to put flesh on these abstractions:

The truth eats its own. (*Verbal Paradise* 11)

There's a meaning between assertions the poem can hardly escape. (*Verbal Paradise* 34)

Language cannot respond to inquiry into its nature without feedback from you. (*Glossodelia Attract* 63)

This meditation on meditation as reading is not premeditated. (*Things Done for Themselves* 41)

It is not the function of language to say what is true. (*The Daimon of the Moment* 10)

In the first and fifth preverbs above, you seem to be positing the truth of limitation itself or limitation of the presumption of truth as (negative?) truth. In the second one, you posit the existence of truth as meaning, but only "between assertions" in a poem, and thus you entertain the speaking/writing subject's possible inability to put that in-between truth into words. In the third preverb, you suggest that metalinguistic truth cannot exist outside of the limitations of individual subjectivity. And the emphasis on lack of premeditation in your meta-meditations indicates that contingency structures the possibilities of truth-effects, thus also questioning the accessibility of (universal, atemporal) "Truth."

I'm aware that my repeated use of the pronoun "you" just now may ascribe a unity of your self and the implied speaker(s) of the preverbs, and that may not be your intention.

I'd love to learn what "kledomantic" might signify, but more importantly, how do you as author/reader of the preverbs above align the play of truth-seeking/awareness of limitation (articulated in the prose of "pre gnoetic") with the thematic dynamics of the actual preverbs?

George Quasha: Thank you for inquiring in a way that allows me to focus on the actual way that preverbs work, which you do by interestingly posing in effect a question-complex with many elements. As such it asks for a like response, an equivalent complex—which is, like the poems or poem-complexes that preverbs form in and beyond the books you mention, not so much non-linear (since we inevitably follow a time-line of some kind in language) as multi-linear—many lines doing many things with their own timing. So, at the onset I have to specify two principles: 1) The axiality of linearity, meaning that every line of thought we may follow has its own axis and turns thought in its own way, which may or may not be consistent with other lines of thought running alongside; consequently, at no point are we building a case in the logical sense but only gathering perspectives and exploring together. 2) The presumption of authorship is itself complex and always in some degree unattested or quasi-attested or ambiguously attested. In short, the nature of authorship is always in question, and the self-reflective nature of the poetic process inevitably thematizes this quest—not, that is, x-characters in search of an author as in the theater frame, but n-texts inquiring into authorship in its nature. All the balls are in the air and if one hits ground it bounces back up.

You acknowledge the second point in mentioning the problematic "you," and of course I'm doing the answering, me as me. But this discourse is not the poem, and I do not represent the poem nor the poem me, because the poetic domain sensitive to *axiality*—let's define the axial for the moment as *radical variability*, variability to the root of the thought—is *linguality*, language reality or language as reality-generator. Poetics is the effort we make to track that generative process and apply it to the thinking we do in any other context. This is not an "art for art's sake" approach since the notion of art or poetry is itself variable, unstable and in question at every point; and the very notion of "for the sake of" is variable. (Nor is it "language poetry" since I'm not part of that historical event directly, and, although I appreciate that phenomenon and enjoy the work of the poets who identify with it, I have for very fundamental reasons chosen to create my own terminology and poetics with no social agreement or authorization as such. Consistency of thought is not inherently virtuous in this approach.) But, as anything I may say is at best perspectival, I am not the authority on the meaning and import of preverbs. They speak for themselves, and I enjoy the process of engaging in their radial effect. I experience them as instructive of my thinking.

I should also say that the question of authorship is conditioned by the process by which preverbs come to be. And addressing this briefly may help with how we think together about preverbs. I do not construct them, and a constructivist theory is inadequate for their nature. I could say I "receive" them but that would imply a sender, which I can't verify or know, even though in certain moments and moods it definitely feels like they're coming from elsewhere. They weave through the kind of thinking I seem to do in response to other thinking/reading, but a preverb comes to be when I feel it happening of its own accord in the mind *and* in the body. I think Robert Duncan said something like that—a certain body tone says the poem is happening, and you follow ("a search in obedience"). I consider that I have about thirty seconds to write it down before it evaporates—and I've lost many through carelessness, not having my notebook to hand, or thinking that it's so vivid that I'll never forget it and of course do; then it haunts me like a dream and I spend hours off and on trying to recall it, and in a sense grieving. They have the strange quality of seeming both mine and wholly other. At times I've thought that they must be somewhat related to the Surrealist practice of automatic writing, but the descriptions of that phenomenon are not like my experience with preverbs, and the sort of wild combination of scarcely related objects has a very different feel from what shows up in preverbs. Likewise my old friend Hannah Weiner's seeing words on your forehead which she'd tell you on the spot! Preverbs seem to want to stay within possible syntactic bounds (inviting thought to try them on), which they violate, perhaps becoming paratactic, through internal multiplicity—more "rule" extension than avoidance.

Let me engage your thinking to guide my own further thought here: *The truth eats its own.*

You say (I translate your "you" to "it"), it seems "to be positing the truth of limitation itself or limitation of the presumption of truth as (negative?) truth." Preverbs engage logic(s) but they never actually "posit" anything, since there's no evident intention to *claim* truth or untruth or even the limitation of truth. Everything is limited and potentially unlimited, or limited until proving unlimited *in one's own mind as reader*. You understand "The truth eats its own" as "positing the truth of limitation itself" etc. which is how it configures in your reading; that's neither right nor wrong as such, but it's interesting to think and contributes to further positioning of (the notion) truth in the mind. The preverb, however, is not doing that; you are. In the preverb truth is eating its own, which when read is configurative however that comes about. I could read it as an "image" of Saturn eating his children (I don't, but I could). I could think, truth can't be fixed because whatever seems true is devoured by its own process of furthering or by life taking it into its digestive system. These are configurations inspired by the preverb. And one formulation that often comes up in my thinking is that preverbs are configurative, just as I say *axial drawings* (on the front covers of all four books of preverbs) are neither figurative nor abstract but configurative. That describes the *optional nature of interpretative viewing*. Axial poems like axial drawings inspire configurative response, which is a *singularity* in the experience of the reader/viewer. We appreciate abstract "form" and we tend to see "figures" or something of both and that's configuration. Axial language creates the opportunity to engage that freedom of configuration within the terms appropriate to the mind at that time. I tend to think that exercising that kind of "freedom" grows something intrinsic to mind and allows language reality to be the site of uncorrupted life process, and even makes possible a world very different from the corrupt one we live in. That's one of my favorite configurations.

The above discussion could be viewed as a process generated by the preverb: *It is not the function of language to say what is true.* That of course plays against the Liar's Paradox ("This is a lie"), and its contrary is equally (un)true. But it's not any one thing and not a game of logical burlesque. It engages actual thinking processes and allows their formulations to live through the very limitations they discover—to "further process" the thinking in a field of language larger than the limitations, perhaps I could say, more open to *lingual psychonautics*.

You ask about *kledomantic*, which is the adjective of *kledomancy*, "divination by keys" understood sometimes as "oracular interpretation of stray remarks," a practice that goes back to ancient times, such as sitting in a room of many people talking and allowing the intersection of phrases to create coherent patterns; it may be viewed as embracing synchronicity. (The ancient Oracle did not make better sense than that; the burden of interpretation is on the listener.) Gertrude Stein is said to have practiced something akin. One could understand this as "chance" in a sense related to the various ways Jackson Mac Low worked—accepting the incursion of language as *guided from within*. And here I have to note that preverbs do not accept the categories "subjective" and "objective," which are reductive almost to the point of uselessness. The "limitation" of "truth" is not mainly a problematic of subjectivity or its opposition to objectivity; neither animal roams the preverbial forest for more than a moment. Language is itself an intersection of "interior" and "exterior," mine and the world's, personal and impersonal, etc. Its nature is radically open. The discipline of preverbs is to remain true to that actual complexity. I sometimes think of Stevens' "The accuracy of accurate letters is an accuracy with respect to the structure of reality."

The above discussion could be a gloss on *There's a meaning between assertions the poem can hardly escape*. Assertion is not the only site of meaning; there are other orders of meaning not discovered by language as assertion or any other familiar "mood." It depends in part on context. And on *level*, in the sense, say, that Newtonian physics is an adequate tool for a mechanical problem but not for a subatomic one. Preverbs extend the permission of poetry to shift levels at any point, indeed continuously as the actual experience of mind does throughout any given 24 hour period. (In this frame a preverb could contain a 24-hour dynamic condensed to under a quarter minute.)

Language cannot respond to inquiry into its nature without feedback from you. There is no language without person; language uses us to journey through its own nature; beings originate (to invoke Buddha's idea)

14

interdependently; life itself is sustained by feedback process which language serves—these are some configurations of the above proverb. You register it in relation to metalinguistics, which is an option that considers the objectification of community in relation to language; at times I follow a related (proto-Bakhtinian) path of thinking. Equally reasonable is a biodynamic dimension: feedback, energy, physical connection between speech act and bodymind, proprioception, and so on. Another perspective is *language is alive and self-generative* in relation to mind activity. We say that we think in language, but we could just as easily say that language thinks in us or through us. In that view poetry does the "higher" or "evolutionary" work of language. I like that view; it gets proverbs excited; they start talking. I register language getting worked up, a certain intensity gathering in the stomach, a sense of energy rising in the cerebral-spinal column and spreading into the thinking hands/fingers ... more favorite configurations. I give myself permission to follow these sudden permissions. I gently restrain my inherited censors. I trust preverbial language to edit itself in process. Trust—an important value within the process—trust of lingual intelligence. The view: I don't *have* this intelligence; I'm *inside* intelligence. And this is a way of elucidating navigation in lingual psychonautics.

There's a "how to read" (to use Pound's formulation) implicit in any poetics. Preverbs alert the mind that the will to interpret may easily become a hunt for ideology, or an unacknowledged effort to reify an ontology beyond its occasion. The preverbial poem doesn't "put things into words" or fail to do that or embody the frustration of the unsayable; it lets words lead mind into "further things." I sometimes characterize this furthering as *the state of poetry*; that state has a kind of feeling tone that seems to come of its own accord, but thinking I know what that means does not produce more poetry. A preverb causes the mind to reflect on its own process, but it does not rest in reflection; there are other things for it to (not) do.

Fink: I want to explore the idea that you "do not construct" preverbs. You hesitate to use the verb "receive," but you do acknowledge that "they weave through" your "thinking... in response to other thinking/reading...." Your receptivity to a host of other conversations and texts is acknowledged as an influence, but this is not the same as a transmission from a single source. You stress the preverb's emergence as a feeling "in the mind *and* in the body." Regarding the latter, you speak of "intensity gathering in the stomach, a sense of energy rising in the cerebral-spinal column and spreading into the thinking hands/fingers," and regarding the former, I wonder if it's internal audition or internal envisionment of the words or both. My other question is if all preverbs that manifest this mental and kinesthetic emergence are kept for inclusion in a poem or if you later make an editorial decision that a particular sentence does not pass muster and will not be included in a poem.

Quasha: Speaking generally about agency in poetry, what actually makes the poem, text-generation is probably best viewed as a sort of continuum, one end of which is deliberate construction, by whatever poetic principle, and the other end something like pure and spontaneous inspiration ("received"), whatever that in fact means. Probably most poetry is at best only approximately positioned somewhere along the continuum, even when it makes definite claims. Preverbs actively contemplate this poetic problem of source and agency, and so I can't take a firm position here without undermining the work's "uncertainty" principle. Yet there's always more to say, which is one reason why the agency issue implicitly or explicitly comes up inside the process of the poems.

I'm interested in the discourse of responding to impossible but necessary questions. My video project of the last thirteen years is relevant here—**art is/poetry is/music is (Speaking Portraits)**—in which I ask artists, poets and musicians to say what it (art/poetry/music) *is*: An impossible question to answer definitively, yet it's one that more or less continuously wants to be answered. We try, we fall short, we try again. The video project, which is very impersonal from my angle, relates to the poetics of preverbs as site of a discourse of indeterminate response. I've interviewed over a thousand artists/poets/musicians in eleven countries (amidst many languages), and my "art" there is in drawing people out to say what hasn't been said. I practice a certain receptiveness and open listening, focusing my mind on enabling them to make their most powerful statements about what "it" is, even as we allow that there isn't really an *it* as fixed object. There's an uncertainty principle at work: *Saying what art is changes what art is.* You ask me interesting difficult and ultimately impossible questions about the poetic process and that inspires new thoughts, and these in turn are reality-generating in my personal sense of what the poetic process is. You become co-creative with my sense of my "own" work—co-configurative within an emergent definitional awareness.

The preverbial interaction with this fact of actual interactivity of minds is to *reflect further*. I often play on Cocteau's film *Orphée* where the oracular radio says "The mirror would do well to reflect further." He draws out the double sense of reflection as both mirroring and self-reflection, as well as reflecting *on*. The dynamic of a preverb, which is always a line and a syntactic unit, contains a particular volatility in reflection, wherein verbal subject and verbal object are in play and interplay. We see ourselves in a mirror and reflect on what we see and, further, on the very fact that we are in a state of reflection, and so on. The preverb is generated out of this dynamic; it's an event of awareness inside language as its medium. As the poet I'm participating in a process of language action that is emergent as a happening within a charged inquiry-declaration.

I realize that this is a paradoxical construction (which may ultimately be the only kind of construction in the preverbial world). Inquiry-declaration/asking-saying. Provisional assertion/assertive provisionality. It's a liminality of distinctions. I experience language asking something of me, an embracing attention, a hands-on response to a demanding condition. Furthermore, I see a connection with the sculpture I've made, "axial stones" (documented and discussed in *Axial Stones: An Art of Precarious Balance* [Berkeley: 2006]): The stones come into radical precarious balance by my becoming the neutral space of listening to them; in a sense I *become* the interactive dynamic between the stones—I'm their momentary ligature. For this to happen I have to treat them with affection and let them guide me, we "converse" sometimes for hours on end. It has an eros, a connecting energy through attraction and response. (Eros, according to Plato, is a daimon, a between-entity connecting men and gods.)

I'm saying all this by way of indicating a modality of engaging the art medium, and I discovered it first in language (starting with Blake). The impulse to say something, speak from an emergent thought, starts the sentence, which in some way shows it has a sort of will of its own; one feels the pull and the rhythm, something like its breathing; its pulse. Instead of marshaling it toward a thought conclusion or conceptualized outcome, one listens in on its dynamic and allows minute adjustments to occur—further attractions to meaning. One discovers what is willing to be said. One is reading inside writing and writing the reading. Much like the speaking portraits (**art is**), the axial stones, and the axial drawing, the discipline of *listening in on* emergent language has a quite impersonal dimension, while of course it's intimately woven through one's personal concerns, experience, reading, thinking, etc. Is this a construction or a reception? Let's admit that these words are failing to account for the complexity of the event. (Complexity here has resonance with the mathematical sense of "chaos" or tracking dynamical systems, or a recent interest of mine, *self-organized criticality* as a model for poetics.) The concept terms we use do their work as far as they go, then comes the time to let go into something further. My sense of discipline is to accept the process and not interfere; an energy is moving forward yet in a state of radial release. A flexible copularity.

You ask whether preverb-making involves "internal audition or internal envisionment of the words or both." Both and more. The whole body is a zone of mind activity. The gut has been called the second brain (see Michael Gershon's *The Second Brain*), and some speak of the heart as a brain (resonating with Chinese and Sufi notions, for instance), and yet we typically think of poetics in cerebral terms alone. Charles Olson proposed *proprioception* (own-grasping) as a key to poetic thinking, a notion which he uses both metaphorically and literally. Physiologically proprioception stands for "unconscious perception of movement and spatial orientation arising from stimuli within the body itself." We move oriented by a complex interaction of factors (stimuli) internal (body) and external (physical space). In a line, a preverb, we get oriented, we get situated by engaging a sensory network and range. I *hear* a line *into* its action which becomes orientational on its own terms and *in* the terms themselves, as if walking through words,

18

indeed *walking words*. They take their (our) steps in their (our) own pre-verbal space. Reading moves through these peripatetic events in a sort of mirroring action, engaging our mirror neurons (reading is doing)—and I see this too as a kind of proprioception. Language is itself proprioceptive inside us. The literal/metaphorical tangle gets woven in the text. The friction of engagement is also erotic.

You ask if I edit and reject lines once they are there. Of course; it's a process of constant (self)refinement. They mostly come whole yet sometimes emerge fragmentarily. For the first few years of preverbs—there were thousands already then—they were constantly coming and going; dropping in, dropping out; and over the years they often changed, but less and less in recent times. I learned how to feel "false flow"—that is, when the excitement of composition would keep on generating more, even when the grounded receptivity had waned. I realized that the preverbial process was teaching me something better than momentum. Momentum is always getting ahead of itself, reaching for what it is not yet; overexcited. Axiality is about staying true to the center. It allows an inner release that clears out debris—a reflective clarity within the swirl of energic invention. There is willing retention, a certain holding back. One hears better. There are many subtle currents of meaning in process which one learns to register. It's a dynamic flow with discriminating awareness. Preverbial space allows for asking-declaring. I've thought of it as a possible mood of grammar—the performative indicative. Zero point composition: Each line gives up the momentum of the previous line and returns to zero.

Fink: In describing how the preverbs are read, you use the term "configuration," which I, perhaps wrongly, would just call "interpretation." Does configuration reflect the compounding of the original figuration of the preverb and the mind/body of the reader, the figure *together with* ("con") the reader's processing? Since you speak later in your response about the importance of context and level in reading preverbs, is configuration re-contextualization or level-shifting of the figure? Or am I missing other resonances in the term configuration?

Quasha: A useful question to make a distinction. There is a big difference between *configuration* and *interpretation*, at least in my usage, although I suppose you could say interpretation is a developed or fixed form of configuration. Let's look at it practically: You pour cream into black coffee and look at it—what do you see? Passively: Enough, not enough, or too much cream. A little more awake to the moment: Wow, what a swirl! Very engaged in seeing: Look, a dragon! That's a range of intensity and concentration in viewing what's at hand. A matter of degree that verges on a difference of kind. There are different species of configuration based on modality of engagement. Some might call seeing "the dragon" an interpretation, but it's quicker than that, very immediate and very brief, changing instantly. Interpretation persists even while seeing the dragon disappear, causing the seeing to stop; alternatively you could ride the process and see further emergence. The dragon-seeing could map onto certain Taoist practices celebrated in ancient Chinese pottery, for instance. This extension of the seeing into an art- or religion-contextualized apperceptive thinking moves in the direction of interpretation; it takes the mind into a thinking process but it also stops the immediacy of perception-experiencing and further configuration. There are of course many micro-stages between these event extremes, and there is *a possible oscillatory engagement* that is its own kind of contemplation—feeling-thinking, thinking-sensing, etc. In normal consciousness we're *after* something and may see something before it's really there (I pour the cream and want to drink my coffee now; the swirl of black and white is little more than a charming delay).

What if we approach this consciously? For instance, I have learned to work certain minute practices within ordinary experience which create the extraordinary experience of what I call *conscious liminality*; the latter allows for an oscillatory intensity/release process that furthers configuration. This gazing level of experience can jump from viewing over into drawing or into language, for instance, wherein it finds a "further nature." If I'm preoccupied, it won't happen; I drink my coffee and move on. If I "space into" the experience, something very special might arise. In this frame of viewing—cream in coffee configuring—I might see nothing, no figuration, just movement. In bigger frames of experience and depending on my mind-set, or more seriously the health state of my organism, there might be a moment of (metaphorically) "apperceptive agnosia" or "failure" of perception; of course if that happens all the time it may be a symptom of cognitive disorder, but I'm focusing on *the fine line between expected order and allowable disorder.*

The brain seems to be hardwired to recognize and interpret anything experienced (part of our evolutionary survival orientation); this keeps us within the limits of biological normality. Blake protested staying within nature's "same dull round over again" because he saw the visionary potential of the "Human Imagination Divine" as going beyond—consciously evolving out of— current human limitations, which among other things sustain human violence and social-political "tyranny" (his word, but more and more our reality). Every act of perception is either a repetitive trap or an opportunity for standing outside past/pattern/limitation (a meaning of "ecstasy" is "standing beside"). This is a long way of saying that the *configurative*, in my usage, is different from interpretative in allowing a self-generating process of *axiality* (on-center experiencing) and *conscious liminality* (the open oscillatory between-experiencing). Together they comprise a single complex principle: Axial-Liminal-Configurative.

You ask if configuration means "the figure *together with* ('con') the reader's processing," and the short answer is yes. Preverbial reading foregrounds reader option. Reading enters a path (a line) and a rhythmic event with multiple options. The lines are, relative to perhaps more familiar poetic lines, quite open to variable emphasis, leading to different meaning-options within an existing range determined by specific semantics, grammar, and suprasegmental phonemic options in saying the line (e.g., light housekeeping vs. lighthouse keeping). All of these lingual vectors are highly variable for the most part throughout preverbs. The lingual array is not arbitrary or manipulative but arises within an evolved preverbial process which axial poetics has taught me over the years to be responsive to. The poem is in waiting for a reader's engagement to take it on a meaning-journey through variably significant territory. There is no final or right interpretation for a preverb, but any interpretation is potentially attractive.

Preverbs are disciples of Blake's phrase: "Every thing possible to be believ'd is an image of the Truth."

Fink: We have already discussed your questioning of authorial authority, but we have not explicitly foregrounded the representation of the self in your preverbs. Since, for Blake, and for you, perception is most valuable as a way of breaking through limitation rather than reinforcing it, one form of exploration that I configure in your books of preverbs is the configuring of possible multiplication of selves, as opposed to the constitution of a unitary self. I could cite many examples, especially from *Things Done for Themselves*, but I'll confine myself to a handful. "Song of itself" (*pace* Whitman) begins with the contrary motions of the emotional awareness of the displacement of an authoritative self or, in Joseph Lease's term "representative I," and a command to a guest to bar access to other guests, other selves: "I showed up feeling I was not the one expected to be seen./ *Welcome to my poem. Lock the door*" (*Things Done for Themselves* 37). Later in the poem, there is both expectation of otherness within the self *and* the paradoxical sense that the comforts of home must somehow stem from this otherness: "I'm expecting. The surface is feeling itself./ You'd have to want to be someone else to feel at home." Language itself occasions awareness of the split(ting) self, like the splitting of the speaker and the spoken, but instead of mourning the loss of unity, instead of being nostalgic, "speech is only natural in the roots" makes this multiplication an occasion for linguistic play:

> Sometimes my language tells me who's speaking and sometimes not.
>   Like now.
> And then. The *I* I count on asks why so secret....
>
> Grammar is getting from here to there strictly between us.
> Identity under open pressure has a mounting weirdness quotient....
>
> Seeing I'm here hears the contrary.
> My thought dangling modifies from behind. (*Glossodelia Attract* 32)

The "mounting weirdness quotient"—for example, in the homonymic synesthesia and grammatical doubling or tripling of the penultimate line above—not only puts simple notions of "identity" "under... pressure" but *opens* identity to betweenness ("between us"). If "my biography invents me in its own image" ("a likely tall tale," *Daimon of the Moment*, 42), then that "image" is like a dangling modifier of "thought" that does not quite accurately join the representation and its object, especially because its object is a process, and any "biography" is a temporary measure.

As you think about poems in these books of preverbs that manifest a preoccupation with shifting notions of identity, how do you account for the persistence of this dynamic? In your configurations, do you align the thinking/feeling of selfhood with other thematic topoi, such as space/time, body/mind, absence/presence, substantiality/insubstantiality? And are you thinking through and perhaps departing from the findings of poetic, philosophical, or other precursors?

Quasha: I'm enjoying your reading of preverbs, and the strange part of the experience is that it takes me in and out of recognizing "my" text, rather refreshing like seeing someone new in the mirror. There's a curious sense of alienation—something like a *Verfremdungseffekt* in the Brechtian sense, a distancing or alienation—"playing in such a way that the audience was hindered from simply identifying itself with the characters in the play," he famously wrote about Chinese acting and what he sought in theater. And this shows me that your reading of texts which I present under my name is something like a performance I attend and cannot fully identify with the players (the lines, the readings)—there's pushback. Your poignant reading is something new for me. I cherish this experience as a kind of demonstration of the principle of the poem: It resists a reader's (in this case *my*) effort to identify with what is being read, to use it personally rather than to stand beyond personal confines. If there's a mimesis in the poetic process it's of something not on the page (the stage) but of an only-now-occurring activity between performance and reception. And unexpectedly this effect points to the way I can address your question about self.

Self is a word-concept for a fundamental but controversial "reality." It is of such complexity that a vast array of philosophical, psychological, social, and religious views could be invoked, and if the preverb process continues long enough, many of those views may strut their stuff on this stage. I may well have believed in many of them for some span of time from moments to years, but now I have preverbs to prevent my attachment to any one of them for more than, perhaps, a line. Yet they can still show up as things "possible to be believed." So a discourse issue here is to what extent I can discuss identity without lapsing into self-generating language which quickly tends toward the preverbial. (Of course an interview, like anything thought or said in life, will have its naturally axial moments that stay in motion even as we grasp them.) Concepts here are placeholders for engaged attention; they're not restful removals from the field of action. I study self, but more from within the moment of awareness grounded in present experience than theoretically. I could mark this a discourse of *self[-]study unfolding in language.*

You ask about "the representation of the self" but of course I should emphasize (what you already know) that it is not quite accurate to say that preverbs *represent.* Or what seems like representation is at best a phase in emergent linguality (reality-generating language). Self is a word-concept that is doing something for the speaker/thinker. The metaphor of an actor on the stage comes to mind again because I have the sense of watching what is happening from some distance. There is a poetic dimension of self that opens up in the process of self-reflection; the poem *gives sign* that it knows what it's doing. At times it seems the poem itself has *self.* It occupies a range between sentience and sapience. Poetic process, as I know it, is not only self-reflective, it's reflexive. *Song of itself.*

To set a sort of meta-context, I point to the sheer complexity of the word *self* in its play throughout language, the way language plays out the possibilities of identity. The *word*-self, the self constituted in word use, performs any social interaction with qualities of the moment, both personal and contextual. Think of Charlie Chan's innovative subject pronoun *Humble self* and its variants— *"Humble countenance merely facing facts."* (Taken out of context this one has preverbial potential!) On another level it's like the problematic of mind seeing itself, or as Alan Watts colorfully observed: "Trying to define yourself is like trying to bite your own teeth." And of course one way or another we the people do this all the time. But we may not be catching our own act. That's a job for poetry.

Your question above, citing lines from three books, illuminates itself quite successfully, pointing to the non-expectation of unity of self and instead occasioning multiplicity and the embrace of inevitable otherness in the site of "identity." Aberrations in grammar (like "dangling modifier") play out possibilities of object relations, given the confusions of subject and object. I see these irregularities as *diversity*, including something like the vital importance of biodiversity as against the life-weakening effects of its loss to monoculture. Prescriptive grammar is functionally a force of anti-diversity and weakens language in part by destabilizing speakers, who are culturally impeded from discovering self-authorization and self-regulation in language. Poetry in this sense, as intrinsically unauthorized, models open reality possibility. Multiplicity of self gives evidence of multiversality (an often more useful idea than universality). Any kind of pre-established authority in language obscures its eco-sensitivity. The destruction of ecosystems begins in flawed and insensitive descriptions of reality, reductive attitudes toward our interactive situatedness on this planet, and indeed in life. We lose our intrinsic ability to engage with diverse living realities, and they in turn lose their voice. We silence "nature" in presuming its silence. *We make things dumb dumbing things down.* (Later proverb)

Multiple selves have multiple idioms. Accordingly I declare a mission in poetry, at least implicitly, to explore language in its widest possibility, which might mean interspecifically. Self itself has interspecies connectivity. Anyone who has lived with animals in any degree of intimacy knows they speak; the linguality in common may involve even more communing than communicating. Poetic space gains unnamed sensitivities from this kind of extra-species resonance. From any perspective other than intimate this level of experience has a high WQ (weirdness quotient).

This level of poetic focus once implied a Romantic lineage, although there are plausible roots as well in the Renaissance (Pico della Mirandola, Giordano Bruno); but now of course it's supported by so-called hard science, in particular ethology with its almost daily revelations of pervasive communication in nature. This is not the place to argue interspecies intelligence, which has interested me since my 20s when I encountered Roger Payne's work on humpback whale songs and John Lilly's *The Mind of the Dolphin*; in my magazine at the time, *Stony Brook*, which launched *ethnopoetics* with Jerome Rothenberg, I tried to find someone to explore a comparable poetic discipline with biopoetic force (I imagined an "ecopoetics," now of course happening, and more), but apparently it was too early or I didn't have the right connections. It's worth noting the popular titles that register the recent shift in biological perspective: Jeremy Narby's *Intelligence in Nature*; Michael Pollan's *The Botany of Desire* and "The Intelligent Plant" (*New Yorker*, December 2013); Daniel Chamovitz's *What a Plant Knows*; and the 2013 PBS film *What Plants Talk About*. Ethnopoetics of course registered preliterate poetries sympathetic to interspecies dynamics, but discovering the implications for a more-than-human or a posthumanist perspective requires a subtler inquiry into how our own language *already* works. In other words, it's not the strange and unfamiliar phenomena that I find most compelling here, but what we do and say that manifests a more complex axiality that redefines us. Our syntax springs leaks that open larger cracks, even windows, onto our broad interconnectedness. Preverbial poetics maintains a certain vigilance for these events of showing through. Self is permeable.

The notions of self and identity come into play throughout proverbs, and each shift in perspective resonates across the others. I sometimes theorize a *logoic butterfly effect*: Every word action in proverbs may affect reading actions throughout the poems, in fact between books. Every word event reconditions the field of word events pervasively. (Perhaps one could think of this as *noespheric resonance*.) It's like pulling one thread in a fabric—the whole fabric pulls into it. We "think body" this way in (hands-on) bodywork (which I have practiced for a few decades and is a source of "axial thinking"): Doing anything to any part of the body impacts the whole. Like the body the poem is organismic on many levels. (I mean this quite a bit more radically than older notions like "organic form," but also not as a limit of formal concepts; it's difficult to imagine a limit to the ways of conceptualizing form.) We impart *self* to language: Whatever is true of ourselves becomes in some way true in our language-making. Whatever self is, it's part of the field and it acts by field. In a sense this is fractal-like in that *self nature* is scale-invariant. It shows up locally and impacts globally.

What I just called axial thinking registers in language for me as preverbs. They happen at times in response to other thinking—you ask if they're "thinking through and perhaps departing from the findings of poetic, philosophical, or other precursors"—yes but serendipitously, book in hand, overhearing a conversation at a neighboring table (kledomanticly), gathering "from the air a live tradition" (Pound, Canto LXXXI), as opposed to a systematic engagement with someone's thought or writing. The practice has a contemplative side, a kind of psychonautics, a centripetal quality of going in and out of balance along an edge, and a sort of slack-rope syntactics while crossing a micro-abyss.

Certain phrases we read stay with us for many years and evolve along a new track, perhaps becoming something that would be unrecognizable to the originator. An example for me would be Stevens' "The poem of the mind in the act of finding/What will suffice...." In my case the notion of "suffice" is indeterminate.

Fink: From the tenuousness and provisional aspect of any configuration of the self, let's move to the topic of love, of communion with an other, which is a significant component of all four preverb books, especially, I think, *Verbal Paradise* and *Things Done for Themselves*. This time, I'll confine myself to one brief example. Here is part of the opening section of "Bottling Up":

She swings in her body tall with these trees.
Almost known is almost to have been....

Words audition.
Is that you calling? I must be overhearing.
Almost knowing, almost being, almost telling.
Flow.
So she shows. (*Verbal Paradise* 31).

Once more, I'm gonna configure for a minute. The "flow" of the erotic frisson in the opening line gives way to epistemological uncertainty. If we cannot know our selves enduringly, if "finding/ what will suffice" of self-knowledge is a process that never reaches total fulfillment, the other, at best, is "almost known." Presumption of total knowledge of the other, total communication with her, and insufficient attention to her and to the relationship as "flow" that "she shows" (as does the lover) are the path to idealization that will breed a deadly, reifying, if tempting immortality, as in a fair amount of love poems and songs in the last few millennia: *"Poetry resists immortality with difficulty.* Like love" (32). Well, Stevens understood the problem of immortality when he titled a section of *Notes Toward a Supreme Fiction* "It Must Change." Poetry must change to stay alive; love must change. "Words" always "audition," because the words can't be assured of getting the part—that is, the attainment of full communication, whatever that would be. The lover here is not presenting a rhetorical question when he apostrophizes the beloved to ask if she is "calling" or calling him. It's an actual question. She might be addressing herself or someone else, and he is merely "overhearing" what is not meant for him, even if she seems to be speaking to him. In no way am I saying that this poem is promulgating a pessimistic view of love and communication but that possibilities of success and failure are built into any structure of utterance ("telling"). Indeed, "No line's too long that lengthens in longing" (33); reaching passionately for the other is "how I know I'm here, and with…" (32).

There is no simple answer to Tina Turner's question, "What's love got to do with it?"—when "it" is your preverbial poetry, or just about anything else. So I'm eager to hear your answer(s) to this impossible question.

Quasha: I'm going to begin responding to this, as you say, "impossible question" in a kind of basic way, because it takes us to the heart of my poetic orientation—with, however, advance apologies to Tina for inadequately answering her question.

"Epistemological uncertainty" is only one kind of uncertainty, which foregrounds our (in)ability to "justify" belief or other levels of assessment. Of course it's pervasive throughout preverbs, but there are other kinds of uncertainty as well—psychological, especially emotional; indeed *ontological*; amongst others. In a general historical perspective Heisenberg's uncertainty principle has destabilizing impact, which may be viewed as inevitable; that's what uncertainty does at any level and in virtually any context. But it's not a negative factor, unless we experience it so; intrinsically it's neither positive nor negative. It's the condition of what can or cannot be known, which might be circumstantial. What is difficult for the mind is to embrace uncertainty and allow the *uncertainty state*, as it were, to teach us; to open us to unfamiliar knowing. Uncertainty can be *initiatic* in that it introduces us to new kinds of awareness which certainty, for all its service to mental stability, occludes. Openness in this sense involves non-resistance, a certain release of grip, and a willingness to at least temporarily *not know*. And not judge. The attitude here is as relevant to the scientist as the meditator. I wish to track its relevance to poetic process and reading.[1]

There are unspecified kinds of uncertainty, unnamed ones that don't fit our available categories. One that I work with could be called *readerly uncertainty*. This shows up simply, for instance, as *what is this I'm reading?* We take a stand on meaning, or at least the operative question, if we do continue on, or else we might give up prematurely. If we have a lot of experience reading a certain type of text we may assume that the meanings make sense in accordance with precedent. But that might not work out. Preverbs work with *not working out*. They embody destabilized meanings

---

[1] I have theorized "Uncertainty" more extensively in a paper of that name on Robert Kelly's "poetics of singularity" in *Talisman: A Journal of Contemporary Poetry and Poetics,* #44 (2016): http://www.talismanmag.net.

and narratives that lead to meaning. My preoccupation with *uncertainty process* is related to what I said earlier: I'm interested in the discourse of responding to impossible but necessary questions. Preverbs declare a certain productive uncertainty in discourse.

This is a warm-up to responding to your highly specified concern that names *love*, and in a sense I could say again everything I said about *self*. It's a word-concept for a fundamental but controversial "reality." And the two go together. We tend to understand loving as something the self does. And of course historically we discriminate different kinds of love, such as the four-love ancient Greek system: simplistically speaking, *agape* ("unconditional love"), *phileo* ("platonic love"), *storge* ("familial love"), and *eros* ("romantic/passionate love," including sexual). And there are other systems, such as the biblical three (minus *storge*) where *agape* takes on the divine-love register. And then there are the Eastern refinements and extensions known as Tantric and Taoist love which are meditative and transformational and bear some relation to Western Alchemy, Hermeticism, etc. I mention this complexity to indicate the prima facie difficulty of simply speaking about love. Preverbs are deeply tuned in to this complexity and often work multiple levels as options of reading a given line, not referentially so much as structurally (syntactic, semantic, etc.).

Which brings me to the "how to read" concern in readerly uncertainty. The Poundian how-to-read presumed a high-culture standard based on preferred historical models, an approach that was in different ways challenged by his contemporaries: for instance, Gertrude Stein, who created unprecedented language processes that caused a suspension, willing or not, of belief *or* disbelief. The initial impact of her work, like that of *Finnegans Wake* or Dada texts, was particular kinds of readerly disruption. So readerly uncertainty is nothing new. But the function of uncertainty varies significantly with different discourse approaches.

I'm interested in the *optionality of meaning*, in part as a way beyond our mostly private fundamentalisms. Take the example you chose. Because the poem images a female person at the beginning (*She swings in her body tall with these trees*) you seem to assume her presence throughout; this is one option. But preverbs are line-intensive and do not promise continuity or narrativity, although these also are configurative options. So the line opening the next quoted stanza—*Words audition*—is held within a progression that has "the lover" apostrophizing "the beloved" and asking "if she is 'calling' or calling him," which you take to be "an actual question," and so on. I can see how a way of reading poetry supports this, and the narrative allows you to consider that the poem is not "promulgating a pessimistic view of love and communication" but allowing "that possibilities of success and failure are built into any structure of utterance ('telling')." I do not approach the poem this way but I do indeed entertain the same conclusion about any structure of utterance. There may be multiple paths to an insight.

It's hard to explain this precisely but I want to say that the sequence of lines isn't constructed so that it "promulgates" something; rather, it allows constructive reading as an option. *Words audition* is quite interestingly glossed by your "words can't be assured of getting the part," which I like a lot (almost a preverb itself). That takes the word "audition," so to speak, at its word. (I do experience words as auditioning during the composition, because often multiple words try to get in.) But there is another way that words come to mean in preverbs, as I suggested earlier with "logoic butterfly effect," which is by *processual context-pressure*. "Audition" appears a number of times throughout preverbs in ways that draw out the etymology as "listening." This is an example of how multiple readings over time produce different word resonance—(to attract readers willing to read this way could be any poet's dream). The fact that preverbs have evolved over a seventeen year period (and inherited many years of axial poems before that, including the long work *Somapoetics* from the early '70s), indicates a basis of this kind of reading. *Lines signify radially* is the principle of meaning-by-field. It points to *multiple reading dimensions*, not layered as coded or referential meaning or allegory, but an actual *text dimensionality,* embodied in language structure.

Returning to the passage you cited (the line following "Words audition"): *"Is that you calling?* I must be overhearing," which you read as a personal question as to whether the beloved is calling—a reasonable assumption within the dimension of the personal. There are other, non-personal dimensions operative here in the "bottling up" of meaning (about love, amongst other things), inquiring as to the status of the text itself, its source, the overlay on or of the personal, the question of (a) "calling" (another strongly field-resonant word), and the implication that poetic reception is a kind of overhearing (kledomanticly again)—whether of the beloved or of something not so easily configured.

Is "calling" the "same" when recurring? Gertrude Stein's repetitive words, phrases and syntactic patterns lead to a discovery that there is no actual repetition, but rather a moving through language that is the opportunity for further insight along a language path of *emergent* awareness. Language is the medium of *telling*; poetics is the evolving guide to help us allow that to happen, unobstructed. The discipline is a gradual tuning in and discovery of a non-controlling-control or principle of self-regulation wherein we learn to let the saying occur as it will. It's in part a discipline of getting out of our own way. We follow a feeling tone inside a language tone, which depending on the poetic modality may be an *actual word sound toning* (like Robert Duncan's use of Pound's "tone-leading of vowels"), a *semantic toning*, and/or something like *syntactic toning*. How much these ideas communicate depends on the particular experience of the reader.

The goal of the poem is to engage the mind so that the poetic principle takes hold and makes a specific kind of reading possible. Depending on the evolving poetics, one hopes the singularity of reading, once made possible, may in the end be powerful for those who get with it. The uncertainty process is characterized by a logoic *jouissance* chastened by disrupted certainty in our cherished interpretations. My experience is that it contributes to alteration of readerly consciousness.

Identity/self/love.... A later preverb says: *I have to learn the faces of face-offs the heart generates.* Instead of a problematic Freudian slip, I follow a language self that "aimlessly" utters self-conflicting emergent sayings while courting life complexity. There is "self" projection the "*I*" doesn't recognize which to "know myself" I have to get to know. Words are masks, ranging between the Greek theater persona to the modern disguise (I grew up on the Lone Ranger; Antigone came later) and on to what in preverbs gets called the *impersona*.

This is admittedly a somewhat difficult art to get oriented to. My memory is that I first discovered this kind of reading in my mid-20s in studying Blake (but it may have actually begun with my intense joy in discovering T.S. Eliot, especially *Four Quartets*, at age 14 while understanding little and not really caring). Poetics in this sense is a species of mindfulness in poetry, the mind tracking its own surrenders, such that neither meta-awareness nor passionate engagement fully dissolves. In the present stage of poetic history this kind of internal dialogue between a poetry and its poetics is not unusual, and it could be viewed as one outcome of T.S. Eliot's post-Metaphysical emphasis on overcoming the "dissociation of sensibilities." One question is how well the mutually corrective balance is kept throughout, and that is difficult to answer, since any new equilibrium of poetic energy and aesthetic judgment is slow in developing in the wake of a truly alive new poetic force. (I hold that it is not the poet's business to worry one's place in history or relative "merit" or who's on first; I agree with Duchamp that judgment belongs to the future.)

I rarely recall what motivated particular preverbs. They are not motivated by my having something to say in the ordinary sense. On a personal level, awareness that includes love is central to my life, but it's not consistently clear how that relates to preverbs, since they're not selling attitudes. I dedicate every book to Susan Quasha (I see her as preverbs' truest reader, along with Charles Stein, from the beginning) but it is not an indication that the *she/her* of the text either is or is not her person. It could be an *aspect* of her mind or perhaps someone else or no *one*; it could be *my* mind since preverbs sometimes appear to identify poetic process as female gender—the "poet"—and one series is called *Fluctuant Gender*. I'm not opposed to seeing the poetic process as in some sense love-sustaining, even eros-centered, and I confess to enjoying, say, Ibn Arabi on "intelligence of the heart." But knowing any of this should not predispose reading to any particular conclusion. *A truth knows its name thanks to its contrary,* says a preverb down the road.

Fink: I'd like to conclude my part of this dialogue by soliciting an important aspect of your sense of the book as book (its "bookness") or perhaps, instead, as "book" under erasure. Although my last two questions were informed by somewhat conventional thematic rubrics, they were merely meant as a point of departure: I did realize (and "certainly" should understand by now!) that multiple contexts engender numerous possibilities of interpretation and defamiliarization for an individual preverb, and the complexity multiplies further when one configures a poem, even more when one configures a book of preverbs. This being said, and acknowledging that you have spoken of an intuitive process of composition, characterized by trial and error, I note that *Glossodelia Attract* and *Things Done for Themselves,* which you characterize as two books in one, both appeared in 2015 and *The Daimon of the Moment* is making its appearance this year (2016), so I can surmise that the chronology of composition does not dictate the architecture of these (separate) books. I wonder whether you as author reached a realization, after the fact or *in medias res,* that there has been a rationale—whether visual or auditory or kinesthetic or multisensory, and undoubtedly rhizomatic—for your decision to gather particular preverb poems into one of these books and others into a second and still others into the third. And if this is the case, can you give us a sense of the contours of that rationale or cluster of perceived patterns, as it might be useful for readers to include a version of your architectural intentionality in the process of their configuring?

Quasha: Again let's go from simplest to more complex. I have a quite precise and unmysterious definition of *book* with respect to preverbs: "A book here is defined as seven 'preverb-complexes' or poem-series of varying length."[2] That structural decision is arbitrary, meaning that it is not symbolic or meaningful

---

[2] Footnote in "pre gloss," *Glossodelia Attract (preverbs).*

but purely practical in that it makes for a convenient and approximate book length overall; and it applies to all ten books to date. A conceptual aspect of preverbs is non-symbolic form; rather, form as fixed container like a wine glass, and it applies to all levels. The first unit is <u>the line</u> (no run-overs) delimited by the word-processing default line (MS Word); the next unit is <u>the page</u>, which in a poem-series is a single poem numbered and titled; then <u>the series</u>, which is the one open distinction—anything from several pages to over thirty, so far. A <u>book</u> is seven poem-series, plus a preface and sometimes a poetics statement at the end (at the beginning uniquely in *Verbal Paradise*). One rationale for these arbitrary units is that it's rather like life: We fit into neutral given structures (60-minute hour, 7-day week, 4-wheel cars, a given body size, a limited lifespan, etc.) and for the most part we make do, since these containers allow for an infinite variety of content and quality of experience. It's a choice, to see it, say, as an enclosed garden (*hortus conclusus*) or to bang against the prison bars.

Beyond that I have a rather minimalist sense of overall design, which allows me to concentrate on intensive language events without dressing them up externally. A seeming exception is that the books have strong visual covers, all using my axial drawings/paintings (Dakini Series) and designed by Susan Quasha. So far all of the publishers have allowed us to follow this approach (Zasterle Press, Marsh Hawk Press, Talisman House Press, and our own Station Hill of Barrytown). But the decision to use what at first glance seems like similar cover art has the heuristic value that people having trouble telling one book from another must pay real attention; then they see the real difference. Same with the interior: Lines ask to be known individually, not because they fit a pattern or are part of a development, narrative, or formal symbolism, but according to the intrinsic event of the line, which is highly variable in rhythm, content, syntax, diction, etc. Everything must speak for itself, without supervening justification. Every line, poem, series, and book asks the reader to be willing to return to zero. No predictable momentum. No overall abstraction as regards style or meaning. No cultural validation by precedent. Everything follows a core minimally definable principle. One of several names I use for the principle is *zero point poetics*, another is *axiality*.

There is minimal "architectural intentionality," to use your term. The architecture, like, say, a geodesic dome, is a structural principle that allows for maximum variability of operative intentionality within a simply defined container. In a sense the principle is scale invariant (short series, long series; short book [*Verbal Paradise*], long book [*Glossodelia Attract*]). And, contrary to your impression, the books are in fact basically chronological within the book but not necessarily from book to book.[3] That is, the poems/series in each book were created in the same time span (say, six months to a year+), and when there are seven series it's a book. The numbered poems within each of the seven series in a book are written in order (though the lines within them may or may not be), but in the final order of the book the series may or may not stay in the order of creation—for no good reason beyond liking it that way. On the whole a book contains poems in series from a single sweep of time; it has a sort of overall atmosphere, which however does not translate into consistency, stylistic or otherwise. So there's no decision necessary about what goes in a given book. Choices are not self-consciously aesthetic or significantly conceptual. They do not "labor to be beautiful" (Yeats); they labor, as in birthing, to allow beauty, potentially "terrible," to be itself without the intervention of taste.

---

[3] The order of the books is mainly circumstantial. In 2010 Manuel Brito of Zasterle Press in the Canary Islands asked for a shorter book which corresponded to the length of the earlier preverb series and books; so the first published book, *Verbal Paradise* (2011), is also the earliest written. Burt Kimmelman made the next connection, with Marsh Hawk Press, and I decided to combine two early shorter books (the 4th and 5th written), *Things Done for Themselves* and *Witnessing the Place Awake,* naming it after the former, and temporarily skipping over the two short intervening books (2nd and 3rd written), still unpublished (*Black Scintillation* and *Eyes Take Away What They See*). Ed Foster then accepted *The Daimon of the Moment* for Talisman House Press, the 7th written, which is the first of the longer books that are now the norm (the intervening 6th, a shorter book, *Listening on a Curve,* still unpublished). *Glossodelia Attract* (the 8th book of preverbs) is the next in line chronologically, which I wanted for Station Hill for personal reasons. There are two subsequent unpublished books, the 9th and 10th (*White Holes* and *Not Even Rabbits Go Down This Hole*). Five longer series from the later books are published as chapbooks in print or online as of February 2016.

This was not all clear from the beginning seventeen years ago, when pre-verbs started out as an accumulation of individually generated lines with no concept of discrete parts beyond collected bunches of lines with titles (a "poem" was over a hundred lines single-spaced and no breaks). That was true for about the first 5,000 lines (some of which did get published online in the first couple of years which I regretted). It evolved, like everything in preverbs, by something like *self-organized criticality* (SOC). That rather specialized physics term was introduced to me a few years ago by the Scottish nano-physicist James Gimzewski (UCLA), working with the artist Victoria Vesna, and it helped me understand how preverbs had evolved from the level of single line to poem to book. Frankly there were important gaps in my retrospective understanding of the uncertainty process which became somewhat clearer when I thought about it using the concept of SOC. Defined technically as "a property of (classes of) dynamical systems that have a critical point as an attractor," it describes an approach to complexity in which a system with many units interacting locally has an unpredictable critical threshold for change globally. Studying the part will not predict the behavior of the whole. Examples include the weather, earthquakes, the global economy, and, recently, brain activity—now poetry. The base is the old but continuously refined idea of *self-organization*, describing overall order emerging out of local interactions, the smaller components of an initially disordered system, or chaos.

I was inspired by Blake's "Proverbs of Hell" in *The Marriage of Heaven and Hell* to trust the space of the line to allow unlimited dynamics, including the transgressive. Persistent progression as accumulation over years began to reveal operative principles which became increasingly self-defining. The important thing was to stay with the process, daily if possible, as a practice, even when it's mystifying or even perplexing—an attitude rather like Keats' "negative capability" (or later for me "positive non-capability"). Quite suddenly a threshold would show up and preverbs crossed over into a new level of organization: Instead of three pages of single-spaced lines, groups formed, eventually stanza-like units of two or more lines. Meanwhile lines would fall away and new ones replace them. Then the next level of sudden organization became the contained page, which after a while took on numbers and, later, titles, followed by series, then books. The process became *intelligent* in its own right, and ordering became articulate in relation to my level of sustained trust in the self-organizing process. It would feel like walking in dense woods and coming to a clearing. Poetic process became a primary teacher, and it interacted with like experience in drawing/painting and music, as well as video. I discovered that art practices based on *principle* rather than cultural precedent or concept can be intimately co-performative.

From the beginning preverbs have come mostly preformed and performative in the ear-mind. I write them in a notebook I carry with me everywhere, ever ready to write because I have about thirty seconds before they recede into the noesphere, back to the wild (perhaps to be picked up on by some other poet). The principle by which lines were and are selected for inclusion in a given poem underway, or for that matter are edited out or reformed during inclusion, I regard as *dowsing*—the pen as doodlebug or divining rod, so to speak, an indicative conduit. You could call it *syntax witching*. I gravitate toward this sort of metaphor of the unexplainable because the process is self-generating, not contrived or rationally focused or adapted for aesthetic effect. It's a nodal event that comes with a body-sense aura, which over time one gets better at distinguishing from mental babble. A sharp incursion of the unknown attractor.

GEORGE QUASHA is a poet, artist, writer, and musician. His work in language, video, drawing, sculpture, sound, and performance explores certain principles activated across mediums. Visual work has been exhibited in galleries and museums, including the Baumgartner Gallery (New York), Slought Foundation (Philadelphia), the Samuel Dorsky Museum of Art (SUNY New Paltz), and the Snite Museum of Art (Notre Dame). His published work includes some twenty books, including, in poetry, the four books of preverbs discussed here, plus *Somapoetics* (Sumac Press, 1973) and *Ainu Dreams,* with Chie Hasegawa (Station Hill Press, 1999); six books of writing on art, including *Axial Stones: An Art of Precarious Balance,* foreword by Carter Ratcliff (North Atlantic Books, 2006) and *An Art of Limina: Gary Hill's Works and Writings,* with Charles Stein, foreword by Lynne Cooke (Ediciones Polígrafa, 2009; expanded edition forthcoming in paperback/ebook from Station Hill), and four anthologies, including *America a Prophecy: A New Reading of American Poetry from Pre-Columbian Times to the Present,* with Jerome Rothenberg (Random House, 1974; Station Hill, 2014) and *The Station Hill Blanchot Reader,* with Charles Stein (Station Hill, 1999). He performs axial music solo and in collaboration with Charles Stein, David Arner, John Beaulieu, and Gary Hill. For his video project *art is/poetry is/music is (Speaking Portraits)* he has recorded over a thousand artists, poets, and musicians in eleven countries (the first book of which is published by PAJ, 2016). Awards include a Guggenheim Fellowship in video art and a National Endowment for the Arts Fellowship in poetry. He lives with artist Susan Quasha in Barrytown, New York, where they publish books at Station Hill of Barrytown.

THOMAS FINK is the author of nine books of poetry—most recently, *Selected Poems and Poetic Series* (Marsh Hawk Press, 2016). He has authored two books of criticism, including *"A Different Sense of Power": Problems of Community in Late-Twentieth Century US Poetry* (Fairleigh Dickinson University Press, 2001), and has coedited two collections of criticism, including *Reading the Difficulties: Dialogues with Contemporary American Innovative Poetry* (University of Alabama Press, 2014). His poem "Yinglish Strophes 9" was selected for *The Best American Poetry 2007* (Scribner's) by Heather McHugh and David Lehman. His paintings hang in various collections. Fink is a professor of English at City University of New York–LaGuardia.